CONTENTS

Introduction 2
1. 1872: The First FA Cup Final 4
2. 1888: League Football Kicks Off 7
3. 1920: Women's Football Banned! 10
4. 1923: The White Horse Final 13
5. 1930: The First World Cup 16
6. 1940: Football In Wartime 19
7. 1958: The Munich Air Disaster 22
8. 1966: England Win The World Cup! 25
9. 1970: Brazil: The Best Team Ever? 28
10. 1991: The Women's World Cup 30
11. 1992: The Premier League Is Born! 32
12. 1998: Football For Everyone 34
13. 2001: The Best In Europe! 38
14. 2021: Heartbreak At Wembley 40
15. 2022: Lionesses Make History! 43

Glossary 46
Index 47

INTRODUCTION

The Big Match: Moments That Made Football

Football is the world's most popular game. Hundreds of millions of people play the game for fun. You can go to any country on Earth and find a game of football to join in with. You can have a conversation about your favourite team or your favourite player with almost anyone you meet.

When people who love football aren't actually playing, they often enjoy watching games. Some teams play in big **stadiums** with space around the pitch where spectators can sit or stand. The crowd makes lots of noise and sometimes the atmosphere is as exciting as the game!

When fans talk about football, they talk about games they've seen and players they've loved. Older fans – mums and dads and grandparents – have lots of memories. They love sharing their stories.

The Big Match: Moments That Made Football is a book of those stories. Each chapter is about a match which helped make football popular, from when football first started …

… right through to today.

If you like football, once you've read this book, you might want to share your own stories. After all, everybody is a part of the game!

1 The First FA Cup Final

People all over the world have played football for hundreds of years, but everybody used to play the game according to their own local rules. In some versions of the game, you could pick the ball up with your hands. In others, you were allowed to kick, barge and trip players from the other team.

So, to simplify things, in 1863, a group of English clubs got together and set up the Football Association (the FA for short). They agreed on one set of rules for everyone to follow, and wrote them down in a big book called *The Laws of The Game*.

A bit later, they came up with the idea for a competition called the Challenge Cup. We call it the FA Cup nowadays. It's the oldest (and best!) knock-out football **tournament** in the world.

The first ever FA Cup Final was played in 1872, at a cricket ground called the Kennington Oval, in South London. Only 12 teams had entered the competition and

just 2000 spectators were in attendance to see a club called Wanderers defeat an army team, Royal Engineers, 1-0.

Nowadays, over 700 teams start in the early rounds. If they get through those, little local league clubs can end up taking on world-famous giants of the game.

TALKING FOOTBALL

8 SEPTEMBER, 1888

PRESTON NORTH END 5 — 2 **BURNLEY**

2 League Football Kicks Off

TALKING FOOTBALL

"I'm an amateur, dear boy. I play football as a hobby."

"I'm a professional, son. I get paid to play football."

Until 1885, all footballers were amateurs. But the biggest clubs wanted to pay the best players to play for them. So, the FA agreed to allow professional football. In 1888, 12 clubs from the north of England and the Midlands agreed amongst themselves to set up the world's first football league.

Mr William McGregor, the Football League's first President

"We'll need a badge, you know!"

"Yes. Very smart indeed!"

The Football League's first badge

Each year, every club in the new Football League played every other club, **home and away**. If you won or drew a game, you got points. If you lost, you didn't get any. After all the matches had been played, whoever had accumulated the most points would be declared the champions. That's how leagues everywhere still work today.

On the opening day of the first season, Preston North End beat Burnley 5-2, and they never looked back. Preston ended up winning the League without losing a single game. They were 'invincible': nobody could beat them.

The Preston Invincibles

We're the moustache champions of 1888 as well!

Preston were a very impressive team and, as well as winning the Football League that year, they also won the FA Cup. That meant they became the first team to do 'The Double', winning the League and the Cup in the same season.

Aston Villa were next to do 'The Double' in 1897. But then it took ages for a team to do it again. Tottenham Hotspur won both trophies in 1961. And since Spurs pulled it off, five other teams have, too: Arsenal, Liverpool, Manchester United, Chelsea and Manchester City. Some of them more than once!

26 DECEMBER, 1920

DICK, KERR LADIES 4 — 0 **ST HELENS LADIES**

3 Women's Football Banned!

Women and girls have always played football. Around 100 years ago, after the First World War, many women worked in factories in the north of England. Some set up their own football teams. They played against other factories, raising money for charity, and huge crowds came to watch. They often played at stadiums belonging to professional men's teams.

Dick, Kerr Ladies

On Boxing Day 1920, 53,000 fans packed into Goodison Park in Liverpool (the home ground of Everton FC), to watch two Lancashire teams. Dick, Kerr Ladies beat St Helens 4-0.

TALKING FOOTBALL

"I'm a striker. I score all the goals."

"I'm a winger. I run up and down the edge of the pitch and kick the ball in towards you, so you can score."

The star player was a 14-year-old winger, Lily Parr, playing for Dick, Kerr Ladies. Lily was a phenomenon, and she's still famous today.

LATEST FOOTBALL NEWS

2019: LILY BECOMES THE FIRST FEMALE PLAYER EVER TO HAVE HER OWN STATUE!

No Girls Allowed!

In 1921, the men at the Football Association banned women's football. They stopped the women's factory teams from playing at official stadiums, claiming that the game was 'quite unsuitable for females'. Maybe they were just worried that the crowds were sometimes bigger for women's games than for men's games!

The FA's decision meant players like Lily Parr couldn't play in front of big crowds any more. It was nearly 50 years until the ban was lifted and the FA apologised. Since then, women's football has gone from strength to strength. Millions of girls play. There are professional women's leagues. It's a game for everyone now!

This game's quite suitable for us, too!

28 APRIL, 1923

BOLTON WANDERERS 2 — 0 **WEST HAM UNITED**

4 The White Horse Final

Wembley Stadium is now established as the home of English football. It opened in 1923 and, that year, the FA Cup Final was played there for the first time. Fans were as excited about seeing the new stadium as they were about watching the game.

Only 125,000 people could fit inside the newly-built Wembley, but twice as many tried to get inside to witness the occasion. Things got out of control. Before the match, there were thousands of people on the pitch, and the Final almost didn't get played.

Are we going to start soon?

How can we? I can't even see the goals!

Then, the king arrived and things calmed down a little. A policeman named George Scorey rode his white police horse, Billy, onto the pitch.

George and Billy gently pushed and prodded at the crowd, convincing the spectators to move back into the **stands**.

At last, the game started. Most people were back in the stands, but some supporters were still squeezed in along the touchlines.

TALKING FOOTBALL

What's the touchline, Dad?

It's the white line along the sides of the pitch. If the ball crosses it, the game stops and then starts again with a **throw-in**. You're standing on the touchline right now, in fact!

The game itself wasn't quite so dramatic. Bolton Wanderers beat West Ham United 2-0, and the man of the match that afternoon wasn't one of the players. It was Billy, the most famous horse in football history. No wonder people still call it 'The White Horse Final'.

30 JULY, 1930		
URUGUAY	4 – 2	ARGENTINA

5 The First World Cup

Football wasn't just the national game in England. It was popular all over the world. FIFA, the organisation in charge of world football, decided to have their own tournament, with different countries playing against each other. The first World Cup was held in Uruguay, in South America, in 1930.

The journey was a long, complicated (and boring!) one for the four European teams who went to play. It took them two weeks to cross the Atlantic Ocean by boat to reach Montevideo, the capital of Uruguay, thousands of miles away.

The *SS Conte Verdi*, loaded with footballers!

None of the European countries made it to the Final, which saw Uruguay take on another South American country, Argentina. Uruguay and Argentina are neighbouring countries and, as often happens with neighbours, there was a fierce **rivalry** between them. They even argued about whose ball to play with.

They're both round, aren't they? Can't we just play?

In the end, it was agreed that Argentina's ball would be used for the first half, and they took a 2-1 lead. But the Uruguayan ball was used in the second half and, playing with that one, the **host nation** scored three times and won the World Cup Final 4-2.

The World Cup trophy was named the 'Jules Rimet Trophy', after the man who was the President of FIFA when the tournament was first played.

Jules Rimet (say: *ree-may*)

It was all my idea, you know!

8 JUNE, 1940

WEST HAM UNITED 1 — 0 BLACKBURN ROVERS

6 Football in Wartime

When the Second World War broke out in 1939, the regular football schedule stopped. Lots of players and football fans went off to join the Army, the Navy or the Royal Air Force. Some were **stationed** in different places around the UK, and others went straight off to fight in Europe.

Children playing football in the streets during wartime.

Bolton Wanderers join the Army

Within a few months, the government decided that football was a good way to keep people's spirits up at home, so special tournaments and wartime leagues were organised.

If they were stationed in England, footballers who were in the armed forces were allowed to play for any club near where they were based. Teams included different 'guest' players each week, so fans never knew who might be playing for their club from one game to the next!

Many grounds were damaged by bombs during the war, and others were used to watch out for air raids or to store military equipment. The national stadium, Wembley, remained in one piece, and kept staging football matches, including wartime cup finals. In the first wartime final, in 1940, West Ham United beat Blackburn Rovers 1-0.

In spite of the danger of bombing raids during the **Blitz**, 40,000 people came to watch the Final. Members of the armed forces were let in for free. The profit raised from sales of all the other tickets was given to war charities. One way or another, football was able to make a difference.

5 FEBRUARY, 1958

| RED STAR BELGRADE | 3 | 3 | MANCHESTER UNITED |

7 The Munich Air Disaster

In the 1950s, a new tournament started. The European Cup gave the best teams from all over Europe the chance to play each other. The first English club to take part was Manchester United. In 1958, United flew to Belgrade, in eastern Europe, to play against a team called Red Star.

United off to Europe

TALKING FOOTBALL

What's this European Cup about?

It's to find out who the champions of Europe are!

Manchester United had a fantastic young team. Many of the players had been at the club together since they were boys. United's manager was Matt Busby, so fans nicknamed them the 'Busby Babes'.

Before the match, in Belgrade

Coming home after the game, the plane had to stop in Munich, Germany, to take on more fuel. Then disaster struck. It was February, still in the depths of winter. There was snow on the runway and the plane crashed as it tried to take off.

23 people, including eight United players, lost their lives, and Matt Busby was seriously injured.

Back in England, people were stunned. The whole country had loved these amazing young players and it felt like a national tragedy. It took Matt Busby and Manchester United a long time to recover. Busby gradually built a new team and, in 1968, United beat the Portuguese champions, Benfica, at Wembley. They became the first English team to win the European Cup. It was a very emotional night for everyone who remembered the Munich air disaster.

Bobby Charlton lifts the trophy at Wembley, 1968. He was one of the crash survivors in 1958.

30 JULY, 1966

ENGLAND 4 — 2 WEST GERMANY

8. England Win The World Cup!

The first World Cup was in 1930, but England didn't bother entering until 1950. In England, people thought their players were the best in the world and didn't need to prove it! In fact, the rest of the world had star players and top quality teams, too. Everybody else had caught up, and it wasn't until 1966 that England did well at a World Cup.

The 1966 tournament was held in England, and a new England manager, Alf Ramsey, had come up with tactics he was sure would win the World Cup.

TALKING FOOTBALL

"What are tactics?"

"Tactics are the plans a manager comes up with to make sure the team beats their opponents."

"Well, I hope Alf's tactics work. It's about time we won a World Cup!"

Ramsey had some excellent players and a very effective style of play. He made sure the England team was hard-working, fast and aggressive.

England won match after match as the tournament progressed. Eventually, they made it to the Final. On a lovely sunny day, Queen Elizabeth II was at Wembley to watch England take on West Germany.

It was a spectacular game. England striker Geoff Hurst was the hero. He was the first player ever to score a **hat-trick** in a World Cup Final. England won the match 4-2, but only after **extra time**. It was a close-run thing!

Since 1966, England supporters have been hoping to see the team win the World Cup again. But nowadays, those fans probably realise there are many other countries who are also very good at football!

21 JUNE, 1970		
BRAZIL	4 — 1	ITALY

9 Brazil: The Best Team Ever?

The 1970 World Cup was held in Mexico, where it was stiflingly hot for the whole tournament. All the games were live on TV, broadcast in colour for the first time. That gave a huge audience the chance to watch what was probably the best World Cup ever.

Brazil is a big country and football is massively popular. It seems as if Brazilians play whenever and wherever they can: on every beach, in every park, at every street corner!

We'll all play in the World Cup one day!

Brazil had a fantastic team in 1970. They were fast, skilful and deadly when it came to scoring goals. They also had the world's best player at the time, Pelé, who was powerful, creative and scored in almost every game.

Pelé – the Best!

My pals are pretty good, too!

In the 1970 Final, Brazil tore Italy apart and won 4-1. The fourth goal was one of the best ever seen at a World Cup: quick passing all the way up the pitch, and then a fierce shot to put the ball in the back of the Italian net. Wow! It was unstoppable.

Fans could see how much the Brazilians enjoyed playing together. No wonder everybody loved watching them in action.

In 1970, Brazil became the world's favourite team!

30 NOVEMBER, 1991

| USA | 2 | 1 | NORWAY |

10 The Women's World Cup

It took a long time for people to take women's football seriously. The first Women's World Cup wasn't held until 1991, 60 years after the first men's World Cup. But it was worth waiting for! The tournament was played in China, and hundreds of thousands of supporters went along.

No, I'm not a player. I'm part of the opening ceremony!

That's 10 goals and counting!

The USA were the strongest team and scored an incredible 23 goals on their way to the final. An American player, Michelle Akers, won the Golden Boot, which is the award for scoring the most goals during a tournament.

The Chinese fans enjoyed the whole World Cup. They weren't just interested in watching their own team. A crowd of 63,000 spectators watched the USA beat Norway 2-1 in the Final. That first tournament was a success, and the Women's World Cup has been played every four years since then.

Nowadays, the matches are shown live on TV, and the audiences are bigger than ever before. Wherever the World Cup is staged, the Americans always have a great team. They've won three more World Cups since that first one in China. That's more than anyone else.

15 AUGUST, 1992

SHEFFIELD UNITED 2 — 1 MANCHESTER UNITED

11 The Premier League Is Born!

There are over 100 professional football clubs in England. Some of them have been famous for over 100 years and have fans worldwide.

"Those were the days!"

"You can't get in without a hat on!"

In the 1970s and 1980s, though, football was struggling to survive. Crowds were getting smaller, and stadiums were becoming run-down. Everything changed in 1992, when 22 of the biggest clubs started their own league. A new TV channel paid lots of money to show the games, which meant the clubs could buy new players and improve their facilities.

It's called the Premier League now, but at first it was called the Premiership.

"OK, ref. Ready when you are!"

The new league kicked off on August 15, 1992. The first goal that day was scored after just five minutes by Sheffield United, who beat Manchester United 2-1. But Manchester United still became champions that season and, since then, they've been champions more often than anyone else.

Because they're watched on TV around the world, the biggest teams and star players are famous everywhere. Many teams outside the Premier League have a tough time though, because they have less money to spend. It's often a battle for those smaller clubs just to survive!

Loyal supporters!

12 Football For Everyone

Nearly one in five people in England live with a disability. A disability is a physical or mental condition which limits a person's movements or senses. But a disability doesn't have stop anyone from enjoying football, either as a spectator or as a player.

Football clubs encourage supporters with disabilities to attend games. Sometimes, disabled fans have a special area with an excellent view of all the action!

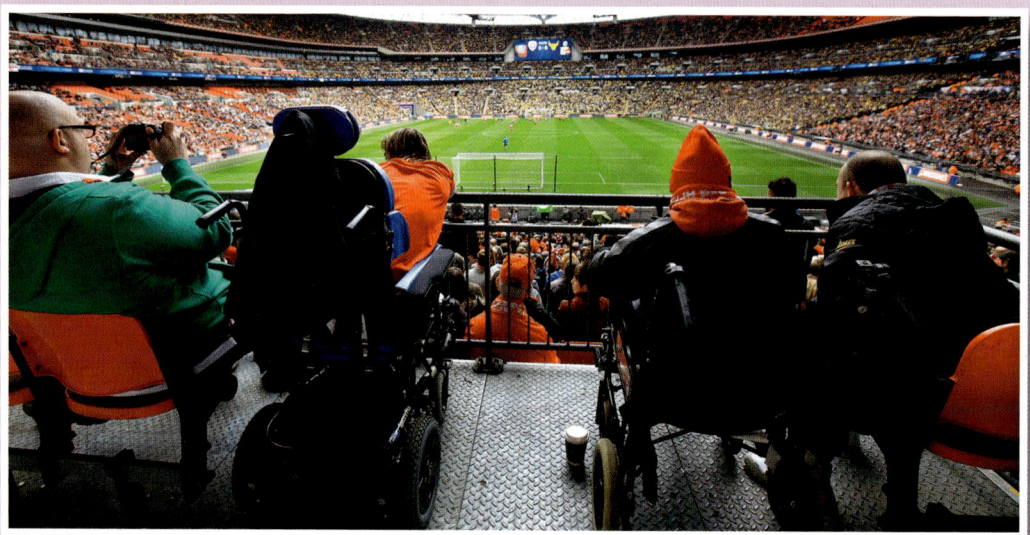

Brazil: World and Paralympic Blind Football Champions

People with disabilities can play football, too. People who are blind or who have low vision, for example, have been playing football for over 100 years. It's only more recently, though, that rules for blind football have been agreed worldwide, and major tournaments have been organised.

Blind football has five players on each team. The goalkeeper is a person who can see. The other players wear blindfolds to make sure everyone's equal. A bell inside the ball tells players where it is. When players go for the ball in a tackle, they call out to let everyone know they're coming!

A World Cup for blind football was first organised in 1998. Only six teams entered the tournament, which was held in Brazil. England teamed up with Scotland, Wales and Northern Ireland to compete as Great Britain. But it was a South American team that won in the end. Brazil beat Argentina 1-0 in the Final. Blind football is now part of the Paralympic Games. The gold medallists in 2020 were Brazil, who beat Argentina 1-0 in the Final. Again. Some things never change!

Football's for everyone. It's easier now for disabled fans to watch games, and rules and conditions can be adapted for disabled people who want to play. Cerebral Palsy football, Powerchair football, Amputee football and Learning Disability football all have world championships now.

Careful. It's a heavy trophy!

No problem. I'll look after it at my house, if you like!

Football clubs encourage supporters with disabilities to attend games. Sometimes, young disabled fans sit right at the front, closer to the action than anyone else!

Cerebral Palsy football

Powerchair football

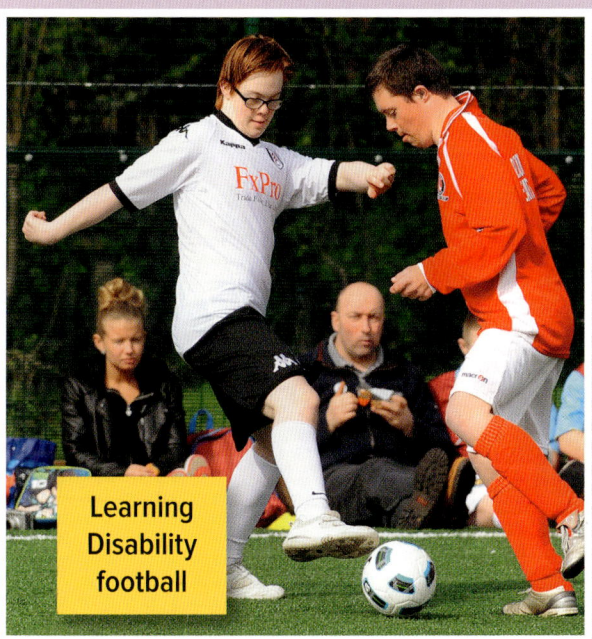

Learning Disability football

Amputee football

37

23 MAY, 2002

FRANKFURT 2 — 0 UMEÅ

13 The Best In Europe!

The men's European Cup, now called the Champions League, began in 1955. A Spanish club, Real Madrid, have won it more often than anyone else.

I think we need a bigger trophy cabinet!

By the start of the 21st century, women's football was becoming more and more popular. A European Cup for women began in 2001. It wasn't written about in newspapers or shown on TV. But it was a start!

In the very first Women's European Cup Final, a German team, Frankfurt, beat a team from Sweden, Umeå (say: *oo-may-ah*). Frankfurt's star that day was Birgit Prinz, one of the best female footballers ever.

On your head, Birgit!

The tournament is now called the Women's Champions League and has grown massively since 2001. All the games are televised. In 2022, over 90,000 fans watched Barcelona beat Wolfsburg 5-1, setting a new crowd record for women's club football.

More girls play football now than ever before, inspired by watching the best female players in the world.

There are professional women **referees**, too, like Stéphanie Frappart from France and Rebecca Welch from England who take charge of men's games as well as women's.

> Calm down, everybody. We're in charge now!

Stéphanie Frappart

Rebecca Welch

11 JULY, 2021

ENGLAND 1 — 1 ITALY

(ITALY WIN 3-2 ON PENALTIES)

14 Heartbreak At Wembley

The coronavirus pandemic began in 2020, and affected the whole world. In Britain and many other countries, people wore masks and stayed away from each other to try and stop the disease from spreading. At first, football shut down completely, and later, matches had to be played in empty stadiums.

The 2020 men's European Championships had to be postponed. They weren't played until the summer of 2021. But the matches were worth waiting for and England got to the Final. Everybody was excited to be able to go to games again. England supporters were even more excited to see the team doing so well!

Come on, England!

The Final was played at Wembley Stadium. It was a huge occasion. England and Italy drew 1-1, before Italy won the penalty shoot-out.

TALKING FOOTBALL

The shoot-out was very tense, and everybody was tired. They'd already played for 90 minutes, and then an extra half-hour to try and settle the game. Three young English players missed penalties: Marcus Rashford, Jadon Sancho and Bukayo Saka. Can you imagine how they felt? They were heart-broken.

Marcus Rashford, after missing his penalty

The worst thing was that, just because they were all black players, they were racially abused online after the game. Most people were very unhappy about that. Marcus, Jadon and Bukayo were representing their country, and they were heroes for England fans. The whole world could see what talented players they were. Why should it matter what colour their skin was?

31 JULY, 2022

ENGLAND 2　1 GERMANY

15 Lionesses Make History!

There are three lions on the England team badge. That's why England's men's team is nicknamed 'The Three Lions' and the women's team is called 'The Lionesses'.

England fans took pride in what the men's team achieved in summer 2021, when they made it to the Final at Wembley Stadium. A year later, in summer 2022, it was the Lionesses' chance to shine. The Women's Euros were played at stadiums all over England.

Fans hoped England's women would do well, but the Lionesses exceeded all expectations. Inspired by Beth Mead, the Golden Boot winner and the Player of the Tournament, they got all the way to the Final.

- 6 games
- 6 goals
- 5 assists
- Wow!!
- Super Beth!

In the Final, England were up against Germany at Wembley in front of 87,192 fans, a new crowd record for a women's Euros match. The game was tight and tense and, with the score tied at 1-1, it went into extra time. Just when it looked like there would be a penalty shoot-out, England's Chloe Kelly stretched out and scored the winning goal.

- Goal!
- Well done, Chloe!
- Yes!

So, the Lionesses became only the second England team ever to win a major tournament. They've changed everything for women's football now, and what they achieved will be part of football history forever.

Bobby Moore, World Cup-winning captain, 1966

Phew! That was a long wait!

Leah Williamson, Euros-winning captain, 2022

The Final in 2022 was the Lionesses' biggest match, and the most recent in our line of dramatic and famous moments that made football. Can you think of any others? Or maybe the best are yet to come!

GLOSSARY

assist — when one player passes the ball to another player, who then scores a goal

Blitz — the German word for 'storm', used as a name for the time when London was bombed heavily in the Second World War

extra time — a football match lasts 90 minutes, but in a Cup Final, if the teams are level, the match continues for an extra 30 minutes to try and find a winner

hat-trick — when one player scores three goals in a match

home and away — a team playing at their own stadium is at 'home'; the visiting team is 'away'

host nation — the team from the country where an international tournament is being played

referee (ref, for short) — the person who makes sure the rules are followed in a match

rivalry — a strong feeling of always wanting to win against a particular person or team, often a neighbour

stadium — the building where football matches take place in front of crowds, with a pitch, places for fans to sit or stand, and changing rooms for the players

stands — the areas in a stadium where fans sit or stand to watch the match

stationed — being based in a particular place when in the armed forces

throw-in — throwing the ball back onto the pitch if it has gone over the lines on the long sides of the pitch during a game

tournament — a competition between football teams to find out which one is the best

INDEX

Alf Ramsey 25–26

Beth Mead 43–44

Billy, the horse 14–15

Birgit Prinz 38

Bobby Charlton 24

Bobby Moore 45

Brazil 28–29, 35, 48

Bukayo Saka 42

Busby Babes 23–24

Champions League (European Cup) 22–24, 38–39

Chloe Kelly 44

coronavirus 40

European Championships (Euros) 40–43

FA 4, 7, 12

FA Cup 4–6, 9, 13–15

FIFA 16, 18

First World War 10

Golden boot 30, 43

Geoff Hurst 27

Jadon Sancho 42

Jules Rimet 18

Leah Williamson 45

Lily Parr 11–12

Lionesses 43–45

Marcus Rashford 42

Matt Busby 23–24

Michelle Akers 30

Munich air disaster 22–24

Pelé 29

Queen Elizabeth II 26

Rebecca Welch 39

Second World War 19–21

Stéphanie Frappart 39

The Double 9

The White Horse Final 13–15

Wembley stadium 6, 13, 21, 24, 26, 40–41, 43, 44

women's football 10–12, 30–31, 38–39, 43–45

World Cup 16–18, 25–27, 28–29, 30–31, 35, 45, 48

NOW ANSWER THE QUESTIONS ...

1. When was the Football Association set up?

2. Look at the photos on page 5. How many differences can you see between one of the first-ever finals and the more recent one?

3. How do clubs win the Football League?

4. Look at the speech bubble on the photograph of the Preston Invincibles (page 9). What is the speech bubble for? Are the words in the speech bubble true?

5. What might have been the reason for the argument over whose ball to use in the 1930 World Cup?

6. What is a 'hat-trick'?

7. Why did Brazil become popular in 1970?

8. Look at Chapter 13 (pages 38–39). How has women's football changed since 2001?

9. What is the connection between the two people in the photographs on page 45?

10. What is the most memorable sports event you have ever seen?